Helping Children See Jesus

ISBN: 978-1-933206-22-6

LIVING BY FAITH
New Testament Volume 38
Hebrews Part 5

Authors: R. Iona Lyster, Doris S. Moose, Maureen Pruit
Illustrator: Frances H. Hertzler
Colorization courtesy of Good Life Ministries, Joshua Day, Charity Parker
Typesetting and Layout: Morgan Melton, Patricia Pope
© 2018 Bible Visuals International

PO Box 153, Akron, PA 17501-0153
Phone: (717) 859-1131
www.biblevisuals.org

All rights reserved. No part of this publication may be reproduced, stored in a retrieval system or transmitted in any form by any means, electronic, mechanical, photocopy, recording or otherwise, without the prior permission of the publisher, except as provided by USA copyright law.

RELATED ITEMS

To access related items (such as activities, memory verse posters and translated texts) please visit our web store at shop.biblevisuals.org and enter 1038 in the search box on the page.

FREE TEXT DOWNLOAD

To access a FREE printable copy of the teaching text (PDF format) in English or other available languages, enter S1038DL in the search box. Add the item to your cart, and use coupon code XTACSV17 at checkout. Once your order is processed you will receive an email with a link to the free download.

Without Faith it is impossible to please God.

Hebrews 11:6a

Lesson 1
THE PROMISES OF FAITH

> **NOTE TO THE TEACHER**
>
> The letter to the Hebrews was written for two reasons:
> 1. To confirm Hebrew Christians in their faith in Christ– the One who is better than Old Testament people, things, and ceremonies.
> 2. To comfort them, by reminding them that the life of faith has always been a life of suffering.
>
> Hebrews 11, which is the subject of our study in this volume, perfectly fits these two purposes of the Epistle. It teaches that all the men and women mentioned had faith. Therefore, they pleased God. Each believed what God said and acted upon it. So they accomplished great things for God. But all of them suffered for their faith. They were often lonely. They were misunderstood. Some were hated. Some were hungry. Many were persecuted. Some were put to death. The way of faith was never easy. God never promised it would be.
>
> Not all of those mentioned in the 11th chapter of Hebrews lived perfectly. They were human–just as we are. However God does not record their failures. He mentions only their faith. So as you teach these lessons, do not give the impression that these people were superhuman. They were special only because of their faith and trust in God. They believed God would keep His promises because He is faithful.

Scripture to be studied: Hebrews 10:38; 11:1-3, 8-19; Romans 4:1-5; Genesis 12:1-9; 15:1-6; 17:15-19; 18:1-22; 21:1-8; 22:1-17

The *aim* of the lesson: To teach that God is faithful to His promises, and He deserves all our trust.

What your students should *know*: Believers are in right standing with God when they trust in His Son.

What your students should *feel*: Confidence in the power of God to keep His promises.

What your students should *do*:
  Unsaved: By faith, receive the Lord Jesus Christ as Saviour.
  Saved: Be willing to do whatever God commands them to do this week.

Lesson outline (for the teacher's and students' notebooks):
1. By faith Abraham obeyed God's command (Hebrews 11:8-10; Genesis 12:1-9).
2. Abraham believed God's promises (Hebrews 11:11; Genesis 15:1-6; 17:15-19).
3. Abraham trusted God's power (Hebrews 11:12; Genesis 21:1-8).
4. Abraham passed the test of faith (Hebrews 11:17-19; Genesis 22:1-17).

The verse to be memorized:

Without faith it is impossible to please [God].
(Hebrews 11:6a)

THE LESSON

Let us suppose it is an extremely hot day. You have been mountain climbing. Your feet ache. Your heart is pounding. Your mouth and lips are so dry you can scarcely speak. You sink to the earth, wishing only for a sip of something cool. At that moment a friend hands you a glass of cold, sparkling water. "Have some water," he says. And you have your wish! You lift the glass to your lips, open your mouth–and immediately close it again.

Turning to your friend you ask, "Are you sure this is water?"

"Yes, I certainly am," he replies. "I brought it along in a canteen." *(Teacher:* Name the kind of container in which your people carry water.)

You drool and look at the water longingly, saying, "It looks like water. You say it really is water. Oh, if only I could feel it is water."

Before you will ever drink that water, what must you have? *(Teacher:* Try to lead your students to the correct answer: *faith.*)

Is it hard for you to understand what faith is? That is because faith is not something you can show to someone. You can show a ball or a bowl of rice. But you cannot say, "Here on the table is my faith." Faith is not a thing. It is believing what we cannot see.

Why is it necessary to understand what faith is? Because God says in Hebrews that to please Him, we must have faith. (See Hebrews 11:6.) God knew we would need help to have an understanding of faith. So He has recorded in His Word the experiences of those who had faith. Many of these people are mentioned in Hebrews 11. One of them, Abraham, lived long, long ago. God asked him to do certain things which Abraham did not understand. Did Abraham trust God? Did he obey Him? Listen carefully!

1. BY FAITH, ABRAHAM OBEYED GOD'S COMMAND
Hebrews 11:8-10; Genesis 12:1-9

Abraham, who lived in the city of Ur, was married to Sarah. As the years went by, their wish for a child did not come true. This made them sad. But they loved Abraham's nephew, Lot, almost as if he was a son to them.

One day (when Abraham was more than 70 years old), God spoke aloud to him. "Abraham," He said, "get out of your country. Go to the land I shall show you."

This was the most surprising thing Abraham had ever heard. He, a businessman, was to uproot himself, leave his home, and start again in a strange land. God did not even name the place where Abraham was to go! Abraham would simply have to trust God for everything: guidance, safety, strength, and happiness.

Show Illustration #1

Abraham did what God told him. With his wife and Lot, Abraham went out, not even knowing where he was going. No wonder Abraham is called "the friend of God." (See James 2:23.) He knew God. And he knew what he must do to please God. He had to leave his homeland. He had to leave his family and friends, for they worshiped idols–gods of wood and stone. The true and living God of Heaven had called Abraham.

So he obeyed, believing God's way is best. He had faith that God would keep His promises.

- 18 -

2. ABRAHAM BELIEVED GOD'S PROMISES
Hebrews 11:11; Genesis 15:1-6; 17:15-19

And what wonderful promises they were! God told Abraham, "I will make your name famous. I will bless you in such a way that you will be a blessing to all the families of the earth." Abraham had no way of understanding the great importance of these words. His child and grandchildren would grow up and have children. Their children would have grandchildren. Finally one day the Lord Jesus Christ would be born into the family of one of Abraham's descendants. (See Matthew 1:1.) And Jesus would bless all nations by His death and resurrection. The whole world would have His offer of eternal salvation. But Abraham lived 2,000 years before Christ came to earth. So, although he did not understand all that God meant, he believed Him.

Show Illustration #2

God also promised Abraham, "I will give you land–much land. I will make you the father of many nations. Abraham, can you count the grains of sand on the seashore? Can you count the number of stars in the sky? No? Neither will it be possible to count all those who will be in your family. For there will be many, many of them."

So Abraham, more than 70 years old, without one child, was promised a huge family. Imagine that!

But God was the One who did the promising. And He can do things which no one else can do. Abraham knew this. So he believed God would do what He said.

God was so pleased with Abraham's faith that He counted him righteous. This means that God announced, "Abraham is in right standing with Me because he believes in Me." (See Genesis 15:6.)

Abraham had taken two big steps. (Show Illustration #1.) He obeyed God's commands without question. (Show Illustration #2.) He believed God would keep His promise and bless him.

3. ABRAHAM TRUSTED GOD'S POWER
Hebrews 11:12; Genesis 21:1-8

Abraham and Sarah had lots of time to practice their faith. Years had passed since God's promises had been given them. Still they had no son. But Abraham continued to believe God. And God was pleased.

By this time, Abraham was age 99 and Sarah was 90. God would have to do a miracle if they were to have a son now.

Again God spoke: "I shall give you a son at this time next

Show Illustration #3

And it happened just as God had said it would. A baby boy, whom they named Isaac, was born to them. Abraham and Sarah were delighted. God had done the impossible.

Why? Because Abraham trusted God–the One who has all power.

4. ABRAHAM PASSED THE TEST OF FAITH
Hebrews 11:17-19; Genesis 22:1-17

Many more years went by. God had given Abraham and Sarah the son they wished for. Would they still be willing to obey God? Did they still have faith in Him?

One day God spoke shocking words to Abraham: "Take your son, your only son Isaac. Go up to Mount Moríah. Offer him there as a sacrifice to Me."

Kill his only son? How could Abraham do such a thing? If Isaac died, how could he have a large family and much blessing? Remember, Abraham had faith. He really trusted God. Quietly he obeyed. He was certain God would keep His promises–even if He had to raise Isaac from the dead to do so. (See Hebrews 11:19.) The next morning, Abraham prepared to follow God's exact instructions. When Isaac asked where the sacrifice was, Abraham answered firmly. "My son, God will provide a sacrifice."

Show Illustration #4

Just as Abraham was about to bring the knife down into Isaac's body, God stopped him. "Do not do it, Abraham," He commanded. "I see you love Me. You trust Me enough to do anything I ask." That moment God provided a ram for the sacrifice. And once again He promised to make Abraham the father of many nations.

Today, more than 4,000 years later, Abraham's and Isaac's descendants are living all over the whole world. God always keeps His promises to those who have faith in Him.

Do you have faith in God? He says, "Believe on the Lord Jesus Christ and you will be saved." (See Acts 16:31.) And, "Whoever believes in the Lord Jesus Christ will not perish, but have eternal life." (See John 3:15.) Again God says, "By grace you are saved through faith; and that not of yourselves: it is the gift of God" (Ephesians 2:8).

God wants you to have his gift of eternal life. He wants you to be saved–safe forever. If you refuse to place your trust in His Son, you will perish. That is, you will be separated from God forever and ever. But if you will believe that Jesus is the Son of God and ask Him to forgive your sin, He will give you His life–everlasting life. (See 1 John 4:15; 5:11-12.) And you will be with the Lord Jesus forever. (See John 14:2-3.) This is His promise to you.

*I have some money here in my hand. (*Teacher:* Name a piece of money that is valuable to your students. Hold it in a tightly closed fist. Do not let them see it.) The first person to come up here, will get it. (It may be necessary, teacher, to repeat your offer. When someone does come, continue to keep the money hidden in your hand.)

Here we have someone. Do you really believe I have (name the amount of money) in my hand? Do you believe I am going to give it to you? You do? Good! For you are right. I do have the money in my hand (show it). I said the first one to come would receive it. Because you believed me, the money is yours. And it is yours to keep. (*Teacher:* Give it to your student.)

What did this student have? Faith. He believed that what I said was true. And anyone who has faith in the Lord Jesus Christ and places his trust in Him will receive eternal life. If you have never accepted the Lord Jesus Christ as your own Saviour from sin, will you do it right now?

The moment you place your trust in Christ, you are born into God's family. (See John 3:3, 7.) In addition to receiving eternal life, God promises other good things. Many promises, however, depend upon your obedience to Him.

For example, the Lord promises (if you are His) to guide you through life. But to have His direction, you must trust in Him with all your heart. You must let others know that you know Him. (See Proverbs 3:5-6.)

God also promises to give you His peace–even in hard places. To have it, you must obey these commands: "Do not worry about anything. Pray about everything. Tell God your needs. Do not forget to thank Him for His answers." (See Philippians 4:6-7; also Isaiah 26:3.)

Are you perfectly willing to obey God in all things? (*Teacher:* You may wish to mention other commands from the Word of God which apply to your group.) How can you obey God's commands today? This week? Write in your notebook what you purpose to do.

*This is part of an excellent object lesson from *Easy-to-Give Object Lessons* by Dr. Charles C. Ryrie, published by Moody Press, Chicago, IL, USA.

Lesson 2
THE HEROES OF FAITH

NOTE TO THE TEACHER

Those mentioned in Hebrews 11 had faith. That is, they believed God and took Him at His word. They might not have understood what God was going to do. But they believed He would do whatever He said. They proved they believed God by obeying Him. Faith always produces action. It accomplishes great things for God.

It is quite possible to believe about God, without believing God. Cain was like that. He believed there was a God. He even worshiped God in his own proud way. But God refused to accept Cain's worship, for Cain did not believe God. He refused to worship God in God's way. He did not acknowledge his sin. He did not offer a blood sacrifice. He did not obey God because he did not believe God. He did not have faith.

Help your class to understand the important difference between believing about God and truly believing Him.

Scripture to be studied: Hebrews 11:4-7, 23-29; Genesis 4:3-12; 5:22-24; 6:1–7:22; Exodus 2:1-15; 12:21; 14:13

The *aim* of the lesson: To teach the importance of living by faith–believing God in everything.

   What your students should *know*: Faith in God affects everything: our worship, our work, the way we live.

   What your students should *feel*: A yearning to depend entirely upon God.

   What your students should *do*: Choose to accept everything–even suffering–by faith.

Lesson outline (for the teacher's and students' notebooks):

1. Like Abel, we should worship God by faith (Hebrews 11:4; Genesis 4:3-12).
2. Like Enoch, we should walk with God by faith (Hebrews 11:5; Genesis 5:22-24).
3. Like Noah, we should work obediently for God by faith (Hebrews 11:7; Genesis 6:1-7:22).
4. Like Moses, we should choose God's way by faith (Hebrews 11:24-27; Exodus 2:1-15; 12:21; 14:13).

The verse to be memorized:

Without faith it is impossible to please [God]. (Hebrews 11:6a)

THE LESSON

When a person dies, the one who conducts the funeral may make a speech. Usually he tells something good which the person did while alive. This helps the family to feel better. If the dead person lived a sinful life, it is hard for the speaker to say something nice.

What is the best thing that can be said about a child of God who dies? (*Teacher:* Have students discuss this.) The most important words are those telling that the person had received forgiveness of sins by placing his/her trust in Jesus Christ. He/she loved God, believed Him, and grew to trust Him more and more.

Why do we say this? Because the Bible says, "Without faith it is impossible to please God" (Hebrews 11:6) and "The just shall live by faith" (Hebrews 10:38). Anyone who trusts in Christ, grows in faith, and becomes a strong servant of God has done the best with his/her life. That person has pleased God!

Will *you* be remembered as a person who believed God and pleased Him?

Perhaps you have heard someone say, "Juan is really clever. He knows how to make something out of nothing." You knew, of course, that the person did not mean exactly what he said. To make his object, Juan may have used some wild flowers, old seeds, or seashells. Because there are so many of these things, they seem like worthless nothings.

But God really did make something out of nothing. He made the whole earth and everything on it. He made the waters and everything in them. He made the heavens, the sun and moon and stars. Simply by speaking, He created our universe. For example, God said, "Let the earth bring forth grass . . . and it was so." (See Genesis 1:3-27.) He made everything out of nothing. (See Hebrews 11:3.)

Do you believe this? If you do, you have faith. You believe that what God says is true. And believing God is the most important thing we can do.

Hebrews 11 is filled with the names of people who believed God. They believed what He said. Together with God they did some marvelous things. Their lives are examples for us to follow. From Abraham (studied in our last lesson) we learn that:

1. Faith is believing God even if we cannot see where He is taking us. (Show illustrations from the first lesson as you review these truths.)
2. Faith is believing God, no matter how impossible His promises may seem.
3. Faith always rests on the promise of God.
4. Faith keeps on believing God.

Are you ready to learn of others whose lives should affect yours? All right, here we go!

1. WE SHOULD WORSHIP GOD BY FAITH
Hebrews 11:4; Genesis 4:3-12

Right from the beginning, God commanded people to worship Him. The worshiper had to tell God about his sins and ask His forgiveness. He offered an animal sacrifice. That animal took the punishment of death which the worshiper should have received. (See Romans 6:23.) The person who truly believed God by worshiping Him obediently, received His forgiveness.

Show Illustration #5

Two brothers, Cain and Abel, knew God's rules and ways. Both knew they had to worship God. Abel did exactly as God commanded. He brought to the altar a perfect animal, killed it, and confessed his sins to God. Because he obeyed God, God accepted his sacrifice and forgave his sins. He was in right standing with God. (See Hebrews 11:4; compare with Romans 10:10.)

Cain worshiped God also. On his altar he piled lovely fruits and vegetables which he had grown. He thought: *How nice they look! Abel's dead animal, with all that blood, looks awful!* But God was not pleased with Cain nor with his offering. For Cain had not obeyed God. He did not believe God. He refused to bring a blood sacrifice. So God would neither accept his worship nor forgive his sins.

Cain was furious! He was angry at God. He was jealous of Abel–so jealous he killed him. Why? Because Abel did things God's way. He had faith. He believed God. He died for doing what was right.

Since that time hundreds–even thousands–have died because they chose to obey God. The life of faith is not always easy. God never promised it would be. Even so, believing God is always the best way.

Today we do not need animal sacrifices as they did in the long ago. All that ended when Christ shed His blood on the cross. Now we are required to place our trust in Him, God the Son. We must tell Him we are sinners, ask His forgiveness, and thank Him for dying in our place. This is what it means to come to God by faith. And when we truly do this, God Himself puts His own righteousness to our account. (See Romans 3:21-28.) By faith in Christ, we are in right standing with God. Think of that!

2. WE SHOULD WALK WITH GOD BY FAITH
Hebrews 11:5; Genesis 5:22-24

Enoch was another of God's men of faith. Enoch loved God. But no one else did. There was no one to encourage him. Those who lived around him were evil. (See Jude 14-15.)

If Enoch wanted to go on loving God, he would have to do so alone. He could not reach out to touch God. He could not see God. But Enoch walked with God by faith. He believed God was his Friend. He believed God would protect him right in the middle of all the sinfulness.

Show Illustration #6

And God gave His light to Enoch, making his life happy and separate from all the evil. Enoch was different from all his neighbors. His actions were different. His thoughts were different. Why? Because he was walking with God. Enoch pleased God so much that God lifted him right out of the sinful world. (See Hebrews 11:5.) He took Enoch to be with Himself forever.

Like Enoch, we live in a world where people do not care about God. Most of them have not placed their trust in Christ. Often we who belong to the Saviour are lonely when we try to please Him. People do not understand us because our thoughts and actions are different. We do not take part in the evil things which others do. But though we may be lonely, we are never alone. For God the Spirit is with us always. (See John 14:16-17.)

Have you trusted in Christ as your Saviour from sin? Are you walking with Him by faith? If so, a day will come when He will take you out of this sinful world. Then you will see Him. You will even be like Him! (See 1 John 3:2.) And you will be with Him forever. (See 1 Thessalonians 4:16-17.)

3. WE SHOULD WORK OBEDIENTLY FOR GOD BY FAITH
Hebrews 11:7; Genesis 6:1–7:22

Another man of faith had to build something different from anything that had ever been built. And he had to build it to protect his family from a kind of storm that had never happened before.

God had determined to put to death all the terribly wicked people who lived on earth. Only one believed God. He alone loved and worshiped God. (See Genesis 6:5-8.) So God purposed to keep him safe.

Calling him by name, God said, "Noah, make a wooden boat three stories high, with rooms in it. I am going to destroy everybody and everything on earth. Only you and your family and the animals you take with you, will be safe in the boat."

Show Illustration #7

Noah had no book of directions to teach him how to build a boat. He had no one to encourage him in his work. But he had instructions from God Himself. (See Genesis 6:14-16.) He had God's words of encouragement. So Noah started building. He worked one day, two days, a week, a month, a whole year. Then two years, five, ten, 25 years he worked and worked and worked. As he worked, he preached, warning those around him to turn away from their sins to God. (See 2 Peter 2:5.) Fifty years, 100 years, 110 years he continued on building and preaching, building and preaching. Finally, after 120 long years, the boat was built and the last sermon preached.

All that time Noah worked by faith. No such boat had ever been built. When God called, "Noah, come into the ark," Noah obeyed by faith. He took his family and the animals, just as God commanded. God shut the door, and then it rained and rained and rained. One day, two days, ten days–40 days and nights it rained. The whole earth was covered with water. Every mountain was covered. But the boat, with Noah and his family, floated safely. Noah had obeyed God and worked by faith. So God records that Noah was in right standing with Him. (See Hebrews 11:7.)

If you have trusted in Christ, you, too, must work for the Lord by faith. You may be asked to do something for Him which you have never tried before. As the Lord helped Noah in his boat building, He will help you. God may ask you to do something that no one else has ever done. If He does, you can be certain He will show you how to do it. That is, if you trust Him to do so. Do you really have faith in God?

These three–Abel, Enoch, Noah–all lived before Abraham (about whom we studied in our last lesson).

4. WE SHOULD CHOOSE GOD'S WAY BY FAITH
Hebrews 11:24-27; Exodus 2:1-15; 12:21;14:13

Moses lived many years after Abraham. Moses had to make a choice that few of us will ever have to make. Should he, the adopted son of a princess, continue to live in the king's palace? Or should he join his own Hebrew people and become one whom the king despised? In the palace Moses could enjoy all the pleasant things money could buy. With his people, he would have a difficult life. Indeed, he would suffer. What a choice to make!

Show Illustration #8

Moses watched the Hebrew slaves receive their cruel lashings. He thought of the good life in the palace. Delicious food, rich treasures, golden idols, servants to attend him. All these were in the palace. But there was more. Sinful pleasures were in the palace. Moses knew all this. He also knew God. And he chose God's way.

Since then, millions of other people have chosen to live God's way by faith. Thousands have suffered and died because of their choice. But not one of those in Heaven today is sorry for chosing God's way.

Suffering is a test of our faith in God. (See 1 Peter 1:7.) Christ proved His love by suffering death on the cross for us. We prove our love for Him when we suffer willingly. The Word of God has this beautiful promise: "If we suffer, we shall also reign with Him" (2 Timothy 2:12).

Are you suffering today because of your faith in God? Do people mock you and laugh at you because you have trusted in the Lord Jesus Christ? Have you been stoned because of your faith? Have you been put out of your home? Are you wandering about, not knowing where to live? Do you know someone who is in prison because of trusting Christ as Saviour? Such experiences are hard, but they are not new. (*Teacher:* Read Hebrews 11:32-40.)

Are you willing to accept by faith whatever God allows? Remember, He is too good to be unkind, and too wise to make mistakes.

Lesson 3
THE FAITH RACE

NOTE TO THE TEACHER

Those whose names are recorded in Hebrews 11 had Biblical faith. They believed God. And believing, they obeyed Him. Some enjoyed marvelous triumphs. (See Hebrews 11:33-35a.) Others suffered dreadfully. (See Hebrews 11:35b-37.) Yet "these all . . . obtained a good report through faith" (v. 39).

It is impossible to please God without faith. (1) Faith in Christ is necessary for salvation. (See Romans 5:1; Ephesians 2:8-9). (2) Prayer to God must be made with faith. (See 1 John 5:14-15.)

The Bible must be read with faith. Faith is being sure of what we may not see or cannot understand. (See Hebrews 11:1.)

In this lesson, we think of life as a race. How can we keep from fainting in the race? God says, "Consider the Lord Jesus who suffered the hatred of sinners. By thinking of Him, you will not faint." (See Hebrews 12:3.) The Lord Jesus gave us our faith and He is the One who makes it perfect. By keeping our eyes on Him, we shall be able to live the life of faith. (See Hebrews 12:1-2.) You may wish to change the names that are used throughout the lesson.

Scripture to be studied: Hebrews 12:1-11

The *aim* of the lesson: To help your students understand that living the Christian life, like racing, is not easy.

- **What your students should *know*:** By deliberately choosing to keep their eyes on the Lord Jesus, their faith will be strengthened and perfected.
- **What your students should *feel*:** A desire to fling aside every weight and sin so that they can please God in their daily lives.
- **What your students should *do*:** Ask God to help them to live so that He will be able to reward them in Heaven.

Lesson outline (for the teacher's and students' notebooks):

1. We must lay aside every weight, every sin (Hebrews 12:1).
2. We must keep our eyes on Jesus (Hebrews 12:2).
3. We need training for the race (Hebrews 12:5-11).
4. Christ rewards those in the faith race (Matthew 16:27; 1 Corinthians 3:12-15; 2 Timothy 4:7-8; James 1:12; Revelation 2:10).

The verse to be memorized:

Without faith it is impossible to please [God]. (Hebrews 11:6a)

THE LESSON

"Sojo, wait for me!" Ballo called.

Sojo slowed his running pace, as Ballo dashed to catch up to him. They ran side by side for a few minutes.

"Where are you running to?" asked Ballo.

"Just over the hill and back."

"Why are you running?" Ballo wanted to know.

"Mr. Kee said we are going to have a race on Saturday. I am getting ready for that by running greater distances each day."

"Can anyone be in the race?" Ballo asked.

"No, it is only for those in Mr. Kee's Bible class."

"Well, then I shall not go any farther with you," Ballo panted. "Stop at my house on the way home. I want to know more about the race."

Later, at Ballo's house, the two sat under a tree talking about the race.

Ballo began, "You were not running very fast. You can never win a race if you go that slowly."

Sojo laughed. "Oh, it is not a race to see who finishes first. This is an endurance race. It is the kind of race Mr. Kee's people have in their village."

"Was Mr. Kee a runner?" Ballo asked.

"Yes, he was the best runner in his tribe," Sojo replied proudly. "He still runs several miles each day. We asked him to teach us to be endurance racers."

"What is an endurance race?" Ballo wanted to know.

"It is a race over a long, hard path. All who *finish* the race without dropping out, are winners. We shall be running on one of the trails Mr. Kee uses."

"Is the trail very long?"

"We do not know," Sojo replied. "Only Mr. Kee knows."

Ballo asked, "Are you afraid of getting lost?"

"No. Mr. Kee knows the way. And we are to keep our eyes on him."

"Why are you having an endurance race?" Ballo asked.

"Mr. Kee wants to teach us about another kind of race–the *Faith Race*. We shall be learning about that at our next Bible class. Want to join us?"

"I've heard of a mile race and a cross country race. But a *Faith Race?* That sounds strange to me," Ballo replied, scratching his head. "I'll come."

A week later Sojo and Ballo went to Mr. Kee's house for the Bible study. The other boys were talking about the prizes they won in the endurance race.

Mr. Kee welcomed Ballo, saying, "We are glad you came."

"He wants to know about the *Faith Race,*" Sojo explained.

"Good!" Mr. Kee responded. "Let's open our Bibles to the twelfth chapter of Hebrews." (*Teacher:* Read Hebrews 12:1-2 aloud.) "Here God is saying that living the Christian life is like running a race–an endurance race. The Christian life is the faith-life. That is, to become a Christian, a person places his trust in Christ–by faith. (See Ephesians 2:8-9.) The person reads the Bible and accepts what it says–by faith. He/she obeys what God tells him/her to do–by faith. That person prays to God–by faith. (See 1 John 5:14-15.) So we are speaking of the Christian life as the *Faith Race*."

Sojo turned to Ballo, explaining, "To have Bible faith means to believe God and take Him at His word. It's like the swinging bridge across the river at the edge of our village. It is fastened to trees at each end. But there are no props in the middle. It looks weak. Yet we do not test it, saying, 'I wonder if it will hold us.' We simply believe it will hold us, walk onto it, and cross to the other side. We have been on it so often, we know it will hold us. That is faith."

Another added, "Faith also means believing God's promises even if they seem impossible."

"Right!" said Mr. Kee. "God has all-power. He can do everything. He has never, ever failed anyone. So we can trust Him perfectly. Now let's see why the Christian life is like a race. What did you learn about an endurance race on Saturday?"

1. WE MUST LAY ASIDE EVERY WEIGHT
Hebrews 12:1

Show Illustration #9

Sojo was the first to answer. "You cannot run if you have a heavy load to carry. And you have to get rid of extra clothing."

"Exactly," Mr. Kee responded. "And the same things are true in the *Faith Race*. Born again children of God must fling aside the weights. Certain things you do or places you go may be weights. Unsaved friends can be weights. Whatever keeps you from becoming more like Christ is a weight. Anyone or anything that kills your desire to read the Bible or pray is a weight. (*Teacher:* Name "weights" that are typical for your students.) And God wants us to throw off every weight."

Mr. Kee continued, "We must also get rid of sin. Not to believe God is sin. To worry is sin. Complaining is sin. Not being thankful is sin. (*Teacher:* Name sins which attack your students.) To enjoy the *Faith Race,* weights and sins must be removed from our lives. These are commands of God Himself."

2. WE MUST KEEP OUR EYES ON JESUS
Hebrews 12:2

One boy, rubbing his stiff, sore legs, announced, "I learned something else on Saturday. Racing is hard."

"Indeed, it is," Mr. Kee agreed. "What kept you going?"

Show Illustration #10

"I kept thinking that if you and the others could do it, so could I."

Mr. Kee smiled. "This is exactly what God tells us about the *Faith Race*. The Christian life is often hard. But then we remember those who have lived before us. And we keep going on. Name some who believed God, even in rough places."

Show Illustration #7

Sojo answered first. "Noah was one. It took him 120 years to build the boat. He preached all that time, but nobody paid attention to him. I guess people thought he was crazy. But he kept right on believing God and obeying Him."

Show Illustration #1

Another boy added, "Things were not easy for old Abraham. He had to leave his country, his family, his friends and go someplace–but he did not know where. He just believed God and obeyed Him. That was not easy. Later on God commanded him to offer his only son Isaac as a sacrifice."

Show Illustration #4

Because Abraham believed God, he was willing to do it. I'm glad God provided a substitute sacrifice. But it must have taken a lot of courage for Abraham to climb the mountain that day."

"It surely did," Mr. Kee declared. "Moses, too, had plenty of hard places.

Show Illustration #8

Once he had to decide whether to live richly in the Egyptian palace or join his people who were slaves. After that, his *Faith Race* had lots and lots of rough places. But believing God and obeying Him kept him going."

Sojo asked, "Mr. Kee, will you please explain the meaning of 'Looking unto Jesus, the author and finisher of our faith'? (See Hebrews 12:2.)

"It is good to think about those who have lived before us. Their lives are helpful examples to us.

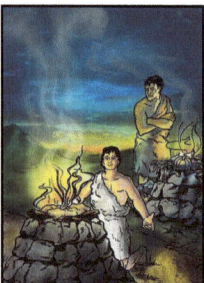
Show Illustration #5
Abel worshiped God by faith.

Show Illustration #6
Enoch walked with God by faith

Show Illustration #7
Noah worked and preached by faith.

Show Illustration #2
Abraham believed God's promises by faith.

Show Illustration #8
Moses chose to suffer by faith.

"But God commands us to look to Jesus and keep our eyes on Him. Faith comes through him, the Author, the Captain, of faith. He is the Captain who leads us to the goal. He leads us when we let Him have first place in our lives. He is the Finisher of faith because He makes our faith complete. He, God the Son, has gone through every rough place in life. And if we keep our eyes on Him, He will lead us through everything."

3. WE NEED TRAINING FOR THE RACE
Hebrews 12:5-11

Mr. Kee asked, "Did you learn something else on Saturday?"

"Sojo did better than the rest of us," Tony answered. "I think it's because he practiced a lot the week before."

"Yes, I did," Sojo agreed. "I was training my body to keep going. I was hoping to get stronger muscles."

"That was good," Mr. Kee said encouragingly. "For the *Faith Race*, we must be trained. Our earthly fathers teach us how to live. They want us to be strong and wise. When we disobey, they punish us. God does this to His children also. Sometimes His training is hard. Sometimes it is painful. But it is always for our good." (See Hebrews 12:5-11.)

Show Illustration #11

Mr. Kee added, "God sometimes sends trouble into our lives. (*Teacher:* Name experiences which God uses to train your students.) We do not welcome hard times. But we must thank God for them. He has sent them because we need to learn to trust Him perfectly. We need to have our faith made stronger. God wants us to become more and more like His Son. He wants us to be strong Christians, full of faith. So He will train us and keep on training us until life is over."

4. CHRIST REWARDS THOSE IN THE FAITH RACE
Matthew 16:27; 1 Corinthians 3:12-15; 2 Timothy 4:7-8; James 1:12; Revelation 2:10

Mr. Kee asked, "What'd you like best about the race?"

The boys grinned. "Getting the prizes!" they chorused.

Mr. Kee laughed. Turning the pages of his Bible, he said, "And there are rewards for those in the *Faith Race*. (Read 2 Timothy 4:7-8.) Each one who looks forward to Christ's coming will get a crown. There is a crown for the person who is faithful all through life. (See Revelation 2:10.) The person who is patient when he is tested and firmly turns from temptations, will receive a crown." (See James 1:12.)

Show Illustration #12

Mr. Kee continued, "The prizes men earn here on earth disappear. They are like the crowns made of leaves which were given to men who raced long ago. They fade and wither. But for those of us who truly believe God, we will receive crowns that last forever. What do you suppose we will do with our crowns? Parade all over Heaven and boast about how many we have? No. We will place them at the feet of the Lord Jesus. That will be our way of thanking Him for giving us faith and for leading us all through life."

What crowns will you receive from the Lord? All who have been born into the family of God are in the *Faith Race*. And we shall continue until life is over. But whether or not we shall receive rewards depends upon how we live the Christian life. (See Matthew 16:27; 1 Corinthians 3:12-15.) Will you list in your notebook anything–any weight, any sin–that will keep you from receiving the rewards God wants you to have? Then we shall pray that your life will be cleansed and changed.

Lesson 4
THE WAY OF FAITH

> **NOTE TO THE TEACHER**
>
> The subject of our study, *Living by Faith*, includes three truths:
> 1. Knowing God. We must know about a person in order to have faith in him. Just so, to have faith in God, we must know him. And we learn of Him through His Word. (See Romans 10:17.) We learn about Him through His Son, the Lord Jesus Christ. Christ shows the love of God. (See 1 John 3:16.) The Holy Spirit who lives within each believer teaches us about God and shows us the will of God.
> 2. Believing God's promises. God has made hundreds of promises to Christians. Because God can be trusted, we believe His promises. We believe Him because He is all powerful. He is able to do everything He promises.
> 3. Trusting ourselves to God. When we know God and His faithfulness, when we believe His promises, we put ourselves into His care. We trust Him with everything. We also trust Him for everything. (See 2 Timothy 1:12.)
>
> Teacher, are you truly living by faith? Do you know God? Do you believe His promises? Do you trust yourself to Him? May it be so!

Scripture to be studied: Hebrews 12:13-17; chapter 13

The *aim* of the lesson: To show that true faith in the Lord Jesus makes us want to help others.

What your students should *know*: They prove their faith by their works of love.

What your students should *feel*: Responsibility for helping others sacrificially.

What your students should *do*: Determine how they can help others this week.

Lesson outline (for the teacher's and students' notebooks):
1. We should be kind to strangers (Hebrews 13:2).
2. We should love other Christians (Hebrews 12:12-13; 13:3, 16-18).
3. We should be faithful to our life partner (Hebrews 13:4).
4. We should be content with what we have (Hebrews 13:5-6).

The verse to be memorized:

Without faith it is impossible to please [God].
(Hebrews 11:6a)

THE LESSON

"I'll race you home," Ballo shouted, as he ran past Sojo.

Sojo and his friends accepted the challenge. "Let's go!" they exclaimed, racing to overtake Ballo. Shortly Abasco, who was ahead, tripped and fell. The others scooted around him. Sojo, hearing his groan, stopped."What happened?" he asked.

"I stumbled when I turned to see how close you all were," Abasco explained.

"Where are you hurt?" asked Sojo.

"My ankle," Abasco answered as he rubbed it. "It's swelling already. See?"

"You better get home so your father can take care of it," Sojo said. "Can you walk?"

Abasco groaned as he tried to put his weight on his foot. "No, it is too sore."

Sojo put his arm around Abasco saying, "Lean on me. I'll help you."

When they arrived in the village the others were worried. "Are you hurt, Abasco?"

Sojo said, "Will someone get Abasco's father? Abasco needs help. His ankle is badly swollen."

Ballo spoke with pity. "I am sorry you are hurt and that I ran past you, Abasco. It is good Sojo helped you."

"I could not have gotten home alone. Sojo, why did you stop? You always seem to help others when they're in trouble."

"That is what Christ wants His followers to do," Sojo answered. "He told us to love other people. Helping those in trouble is one way to show our love for them."

The other boys were listening. Sojo continued, "When we think of all Jesus does to help us, we want to help others. Tomorrow at Bible class we shall be studying about helping others in the *Faith Race*. Would any of you like to come?" The boys all nodded yes.

The next afternoon, Sojo and Abasco came to class slowly. Abasco, with bandaged ankle, was leaning on Sojo. Mr. Kee welcomed them asking, "How is your ankle, Abasco?"

Abasco grinned. "Sore! But my father says it will get better. It's good Sojo was there to help me get home."

Turning in his Bible, Mr. Kee smiled at Sojo. "I think you helped us to understand two verses in the book of Hebrews." (Read Hebrews 12:12-13.) "I am sure that in the future all of us will be more careful to help others in trouble."

Mr. Kee continued, "Last week we spoke of the *Faith Race*. What kind of race is it?"

Tony answered, "An endurance race. We all tried to finish the race. It did not matter who got to the end first. Yesterday our race was different. We were trying to beat others."

Mr. Kee agreed. "In the endurance race, speed is not important. We keep right on going until we finish. If yesterday's race had been an endurance race, even Abasco and Sojo would have won. They got home later, but they did get home. They finished the race."

Mr. Kee continued, "Today we want to talk about helping others. The verses I just read teach about helping those who are weak and lame. Those who are stronger are not to run off and leave the weaker ones. They are to help them along, as Sojo helped Abasco yesterday."

"How else can we help others in the *Faith Race*?" one boy wanted to know.

1. WE SHOULD BE KIND TO STRANGERS
Hebrews 13:2

"God lists many ways in Hebrews 13," Mr. Kee answered. "For example, we should show kindness and love to strangers. Some who have done this have even entertained angels without knowing it!" (See Hebrews 13:2.)

"Angels?" a curious boy asked. "Who ever entertained angels without knowing it?"

Mr. Kee replied, "God records in His Word that Abraham had that experience."

Mr. Kee continued, "One day, old Abraham (he was almost 100 years old) was sitting at the door of his tent. (See Genesis 18:1-10.) Looking into the distance, he saw three strangers coming his way. He knew God wanted him to be kind to strangers. So he rushed to meet them.

Show Illustration #13

"He invited them to rest under the tree, while he got them water to wash their feet. He hurried into the tent, asking his wife to get some food ready. And he ran to the herd and chose a calf for meat. Although these men were strangers, he treated them as he would have treated his best friends."

"Were they angels?" asked one of the boys.

"Yes, they were messengers sent from God. They told Abraham and Sarah that the son God had promised them would be born the next year. And listen to this! One of those three was the Lord Himself! Do you think Abraham was glad he treated the visitors well? Doing things for others is like doing them for the Lord." (See Matthew 25:34-45.)

2. WE SHOULD LOVE OTHER CHRISTIANS
Hebrews 12:12-13; 13:3, 16-18

Mr. Kee continued, "The Lord Jesus tells us we can do something to show we belong to Him. He said, 'All men will know you are My followers (disciples) if you love one another.' (See John 13:35.) He commands: 'Love one another, as I have loved you' (John 13:34)."

"God says, 'Keep loving your Christian brothers and sisters' (Hebrews 13:1) and 'Do good and share, for with this kind of sacrifice God is well pleased' (Hebrews 13:16). Is there someone who needs your help? Do you have something you can share with that person this week?" (*Teacher:* Have class discussion.)

"God also commands us to help those in bonds or in adversity (Hebrews 13:3). Who would they be?" Mr. Kee asked.

Ballo raised his hand. "Does He mean people who are prisoners or who are being punishments?"

Show Illustration #14

"Exactly! At the time this letter was written to the Hebrews, many Christians needed comfort. They were suffering in prison because they had told others about their faith in Christ. It took love and courage for other Christians to visit the prisoners. If they were caught, they, too, were in danger of being thrown into prison."

Sojo spoke up. "Even if we cannot visit those in prison, we can pray for them."

"Good thinking," Mr. Kee responded. "We must pray also for our church leaders.' (See Hebrews 13:7, 17. *Teacher:* Name leaders in your church whom the students know. If possible, stop at this point in the lesson and pray for them right now.)

3. WE SHOULD BE FAITHFUL TO OUR LIFE PARTNER
Hebrews 13:4

Show Illustration #15

"God commands us to be true to the one we marry." (See Hebrews 13:4).

Abasco spoke up. "I know some husbands and wives who are not true to each other."

"I am sorry that is so," Mr. Kee replied. "God says that when a man and woman get married they are one for life. They may be tempted by others. (See Matthew 19:3-6.) Study the illustration. Do you see women trying to distract the man in the center who is joined to his wife? Men (even an old man with a cane!) are trying to attract the woman and get her away from her husband.

One of the boys giggled. "We are too young to be married."

Mr. Kee looked serious. "Some day you will choose a wife. And God says it is sinful for a Christian to marry one who is not a Christian (1 Corinthians 7:39). So even now while you are young, you should begin asking God to help you choose the right partner."

4. WE SHOULD BE CONTENT WITH WHAT WE HAVE
Hebrews 13:5-6

"Here is another command which will help us in the *Faith Race*. God says 'Be content with such things as you have . . .' (Hebrews 3:5). Perhaps this is the hardest of all for all of us. We always want more than we have. It is easy to become jealous of others when they have more than we do. Sometimes we feel sorry for ourselves because others have something better than we have. It takes faith to believe that God knows exactly how much is best for us."

Mr. Kee continued, "Two of Abraham's grandsons, Jacob and Esau, were discontented."

Show Illustration #16

"Esau came in from hunting one day. He had not been able to kill anything and he was hungry. His brother Jacob was cooking a meal. Smelling the good food, Esau said, 'Give me some.'"

"Jacob was a schemer. He thought to himself, *Here's my chance to get Esau's special rights.* (Esau, being older, would receive special family rights. Jacob, because he was younger, was not entitled to them, but he wanted what belonged to Esau.)

"Neither Jacob nor Esau was content with what he had. Jacob wanted Esau's special family rights. And Esau wanted the meal Jacob was cooking. Esau did not really care about the promises of family blessings. He was much more interested in food. So he agreed to trade all of the special blessings for a meal.

"Later, Esau hated himself for having made the trade. He hated Jacob because Jacob had tricked him. In time, Jacob had to leave his home and family for many years. He was certain Esau hated him enough to kill him. What a shame! The whole family was torn apart because neither son was content with what he had. We cause ourselves–and others–much sorrow when we are not content with what we have."

In these lessons, we have learned that faith is believing God and taking Him at His word. Faith is believing God's promises even when they seem impossible. We have learned that it takes faith to worship God, to walk with Him, to work for Him, and to choose His way. We have seen that the Christian life is like an endurance race. In it, we all run with our eyes on Jesus. He is the One who planned our lives for us. He has gone ahead and shown us how to live the Christian life.

Today, we learned that we should help others as they run the *Faith Race*. When we share with others sacrificially, God is well pleased. He has promised rewards to those who run the race well and finish the course. And we are to be content with what we have.

There is someone whom you know, surely, who needs your help this week. You may have to give up your own time or some of your money in order to help that person. Are you willing to do this? Will you share yourself and what you have with someone else? Write that person's name in your notebook. Include what you think God wants you to do for him/her/them this week. Then we shall pray that God will help you to do this.

www.ingramcontent.com/pod-product-compliance
Lightning Source LLC
Chambersburg PA
CBHW060804090426
42736CB00002B/156